Doing More with Less:

The Art of Working Smart"

Cecilia. N. Johnson

Table of contents

.Introduction

Resource Optimization

Creativity and Innovation

Lean Management Principles

.Agile Methodologies

Case Studies

.Team Collaboration

1.Introduction

The Concept of "Doing More with Less"
Doing More with Less" is a powerful concept that's becoming increasingly relevant in today's world, as people are realizing that working harder doesn't necessarily lead to greater results. Instead, working smarter and streamlining your tasks is key to achieving more with less effort. In this book, you'll learn how to identify and eliminate inefficiencies, streamline your workflows, automate repetitive tasks, and make the most of your time. You'll also learn how to say "no" to things that don't align with your priorities, so you can focus on the things that truly matter.
This early version of Pi can make mistakes. Please don't rely on its information.

Importance and BenefitsThe concept of "doing more with less" is important for several reasons. First, it can help you achieve greater results with less stress and burnout. Second, it can give you more time to focus on the things that truly matter to you, whether that's family, friends, hobbies, or personal growth. Third, it can help you become more efficient and productive, which can boost your career and improve your overall quality of life. Finally, it can lead to a sense of fulfillment and satisfaction, knowing that you're making the most of your time and resources

2.Strategies for Efficiency

There are many strategies you can use to become more efficient and do more with less. One strategy is the Pareto Principle, also known as the 80/20 rule. This states that 80% of your results come from 20% of your efforts. So, if you can identify the 20% of tasks that are most important and focus on those, you can maximize your results with minimal effort. Another strategy is the "Eat That Frog" method, which encourages you to tackle the most difficult or unpleasant tasks first, so you can get them out of the way and focus on the easier tasks later

Streamlining Processes and Workflows

Streamlining processes and workflows is a great way to do more with less. It involves identifying and eliminating unnecessary steps in your processes, automating repetitive tasks, and standardizing tasks to make them more efficient. One way to streamline your workflows is to create a process map, which is a visual representation of all the steps involved in a task or project. This can help you identify inefficiencies and streamline the process. Another strategy is to use tools like automation software, which can automate repetitive tasks and save you time.

Automation and Technology Integration Automation and technology integration are crucial elements of the "do more with less" approach. With the right automation tools, you can eliminate manual data entry, improve accuracy, and save time. For example, you can use a tool like Zapier to automatically transfer data from one app to another, or use a chatbot to handle simple customer service inquiries. Additionally, integrating different software tools can improve efficiency by reducing the need to switch between apps and manually transfer data. This can reduce human error and save you a lot of time in the long run.

Prioritization and Time Management

Prioritization and time management are crucial skills for anyone looking to do more with less. With good time management, you can make sure you're focusing on the tasks that matter most and not wasting time on less important tasks. Some strategies for better time management include:

Creating a daily to-do list with only the most important tasks

Blocking out time for important tasks on your calendar

Scheduling time for breaks and self-care

Saying "no" to unimportant tasks or requests that will take time away from your priorities.

Resource Optimization

In addition to time management, it's also important to optimize your use of other resources. This includes using your physical space, technology, and money as efficiently as possible. For example, you can optimize your physical space by decluttering and organizing it, so you can easily find what you need and eliminate distractions. You can also use technology to help you save time and money, such as using cloud-based storage to keep important files organized and accessible from anywhere. Finally, you can save money by finding cheaper alternatives for expensive products or services, or by negotiating better prices.

Maximizing Resource Utilization already have. This involves not only using your resources efficiently, but also finding ways to make the most of them. For example, you can:

Utilize free or low-cost resources available online, such as tutorials, webinars, or courses.

Repurpose existing content, such as turning a blog post into an infographic or social media post.

Make use of collaborative tools to make the most of your team's talents and skills.

Reducing Waste and Overhead

Reducing waste and overhead costs can also be a great way to do more with less. This involves identifying and eliminating unnecessary or duplicated processes, materials, or expenses. For example, you can:

Review your processes and look for inefficiencies or redundancies.

Conduct an inventory of supplies and get rid of anything that's not needed or expired.

Negotiate better rates with vendors or suppliers.

Consider using more sustainable materials and practices to reduce waste and environmental impact.

This early version of Pi can make mistakes. Please don't rely on its information.

Leveraging Available Tools and Assets

Another strategy for doing more with less is to leverage the tools and assets you already have. This can include:

Using the features of existing software or hardware to their fullest potential.

Taking advantage of free or low-cost features that you might not be aware of.

Reusing or repurposing old assets, like furniture or supplies.

Finding creative ways to use the resources you have, such as crowdsourcing ideas from your team or customers.

Harnessing the power of partnerships and collaboration with other organizations

Creativity and Innovation

Creativity and innovation are also essential for doing more with less. With a bit of creativity, you can often find new solutions or approaches to problems that will save you time, money, and resources. Some examples include:

Brainstorming with others to come up with new ideas.

Embracing failure as an opportunity to learn and improve.

Taking risks and trying new things.

Being open to learning and adapting as you go.

Encouraging an environment of creativity and innovation in your team or organization.

Finding Innovative Solutions

way of thinking. Instead of approaching problems from a traditional perspective, try to approach them from new angles. For example:

Ask "what if" questions to imagine new possibilities.

Imagine how you would solve the problem if you had unlimited resources.

Put yourself in the shoes of others, such as your customers or your team members.

Question assumptions and challenge the status quo.

Look to other industries for inspiration.

Embrace diversity of thought by seeking input from a diverse group of people.

Encouraging Creative Thinking

innovative solutions. To do this, you can:

Encourage team members to voice their ideas, even if they seem outlandish.

Create a psychologically safe environment where people feel comfortable sharing their ideas without fear of judgment.

Hold brainstorming sessions where everyone is encouraged to think outside the box.

Promote experimentation and learning from failures.

Celebrate successes and acknowledge innovative efforts, even when they don't have immediate results.

Provide time and resources for people to experiment and explore new ideas.

Adapting to Constraints

It's also important to remember that constraints can be a source of creativity and innovation. For example, necessity is often the mother of invention - some of the best solutions are born out of limited resources. With this in mind, here are some tips for adapting to constraints:

Embrace constraints as a creative challenge.

Look for opportunities within constraints.

Take a fresh look at the constraints to identify hidden opportunities.

Focus on what is possible, rather than what is not possible.

Think of constraints as a source of inspiration and innovation.

Be open to unexpected results.

principles. Lean management is all about eliminating waste and improving efficiency. Some key lean management principles that can help you do more with less include:

Value - understanding what your customers really value.

Value stream - identifying all the steps that go into delivering the value that your customers want.

Flow - eliminating anything that stops the value stream from flowing smoothly.

Pull - producing only what is needed, when it is needed.

Perfection - constantly striving to improve and eliminate waste.

This early version of Pi can make mistakes. Please don't rely on its information.

Introduction to Lean Thinking

Lean thinking is a way of looking at the world that focuses on maximizing value and minimizing waste. It's based on the idea that any activity that doesn't add value for the customer Is a form of waste. By eliminating waste, lean thinking aims to create more value for the customer with fewer resources. Lean thinking can be applied to any process or organization, from manufacturing to healthcare to software development. It has its roots in the Toyota Production System and has been widely adopted by organizations around the world.

Eliminating Non-Value-Adding Activities

value-adding activities, or waste. There are seven categories of waste in lean thinking:

Defects: activities that lead to defects or errors in the product or process.

Overproduction: producing more than is needed or in advance of demand.

Waiting: processes that involve long wait times or delays.

Transportation: moving things unnecessarily or inefficiently.

Inventory: holding too much inventory or raw materials.

Motion: unnecessary movement or travel.

Over-processing: performing tasks or using resources that aren't needed

Continuous Improvement

Once you've identified and eliminated waste, the next step is to continuously improve your processes. This is known as kaizen, the Japanese word for "improvement" or "change for the better". Kaizen is a never-ending process of making small, incremental improvements that eventually lead to big changes. To achieve kaizen, organizations must create a culture of continuous learning and improvement, in which everyone is encouraged to find better ways of doing things. This includes identifying problems, analyzing them, and implementing solutions

.Agile Methodologies

Agile methodologies are a set of practices and principles that are heavily influenced by lean thinking. Agile is most commonly used in software development, but it can be applied to other areas as well. The main idea behind agile is to break down large projects into smaller, manageable chunks and to deliver value to the customer as early as possible. Agile teams work in short cycles, called sprints, during which they focus on delivering a specific piece of functionality. Agile teams also use regular feedback and reflection to continuously improve their processes.

Introduction to Agile

Agile development was first described in the Agile Manifesto, a document written in 2001 by a group of software developers who wanted to find a better way to develop software. They were frustrated with traditional "waterfall" development methods, which were slow, inflexible, and often resulted in products that didn't meet the needs of customers. In contrast, agile methods are designed to be flexible, fast, and customer-focused. They're based on a set of values and principles that emphasize collaboration, adaptability, and continual improvement.

Agile Project Management

Agile project management is the process of applying agile values and principles to the management of projects. It involves breaking a project down into smaller, manageable chunks and focusing on delivering value to the customer at each step. Agile project management involves four key stages:

Sprint planning: breaking down the project into sprints and deciding which features to deliver in each one.

Sprint execution: the team works on implementing the features for the current sprint.

Sprint review: at the end of each sprint, the team presents the work to the customer for feedback.

Flexibility and Adaptability

Flexibility and adaptability are key features of agile project management. The team must be able to quickly adapt to changing requirements and priorities. This is achieved through regular communication and collaboration with the customer, so the team can respond quickly to their needs. Agile teams also use a technique called "timeboxing" to ensure they stay on track. Each task is given a fixed amount of time in which it must be completed. This encourages the team to work efficiently and focus on the most important tasks. It also prevents scope creep, the tendency for projects to grow and become more complex over time

Case Studies

There are many successful case studies of agile project management. One famous example is that of the development of the first version of the Spotify music streaming app. The team used agile methods to develop and release the app quickly, despite constantly changing requirements and a fast-paced development environment. The Spotify team attributes the success of the project to their use of agile principles, such as collaboration, continuous improvement, and timeboxing. As a result, they were able to deliver a high-quality product that satisfied the needs of their customers

Real-world Examples of "Doing More with Less"
There are many real-world examples of businesses and organizations who have found success by doing more with less. One well-known example is Netflix. In the early days of the company, they experimented with different business models, and eventually found success with their subscription-based streaming model. This allowed them to reduce the need for physical infrastructure, such as DVD warehouses and delivery services. As a result, they were able to save money and focus on the core of their business: providing customers with quality content. Other companies who have found success with a similar approach include Airbnb, Amazon, and Uber

Lessons Learned and Takeaways

There are many important lessons to be learned from these examples. First, it's important to experiment and be open to change. These companies were willing to pivot their business models and try new approaches. Second, focus on the core of your business and eliminate unnecessary complexity. Third, look for ways to use technology to simplify processes and reduce costs. And finally, always keep the customer at the center of your decisions. By putting the customer first, you can create a product or service that truly meets their needs

.Team Collaboration

In *addition to these lessons, it's also important to consider the role of team collaboration in agile project management. The success of agile teams is often attributed to the fact that they work together as a cohesive unit, rather than in silos. This collaboration is fostered through regular communication and shared goals. Each team member is encouraged to provide input and share their ideas. This type of collaboration leads to increased efficiency, creativity, and motivation. The result is a team that is committed to delivering the best possible product or service to the customer*

Effective Communication and Collaboration

Effective communication and collaboration are key to the success of an agile team. The communication should be regular, transparent, and two-way. This means that everyone should be able to share their thoughts and ideas freely, and that everyone should listen to and consider these ideas. In terms of collaboration, the team should have a shared vision and common goals. This helps to ensure that everyone is working towards the same outcome. They should also have a culture of trust and respect, which allows team members to feel comfortable sharing their opinions and giving honest feedback.

Cross-functional Teams

another important characteristic of successful agile teams is cross-functionality. This means that the team has a diverse set of skills and perspectives, which helps them to approach problems from different angles and come up with creative solutions. For example, a cross-functional team might include a developer, a designer, a tester, and a marketer. Each person brings a different perspective and set of skills to the table, which can lead to a better final product. This diversity also helps to avoid groupthink and tunnel vision.

Fostering a Collaborative Culture

Creating a culture of collaboration is essential for agile teams to succeed. Leaders can foster this culture in a number of ways. First, they should lead by example. Leaders should be open and transparent, and should be willing to seek input from team members. Second, leaders should provide the right tools and resources to support collaboration. This might include a shared online workspace, a tool for tracking progress, and a culture of open communication. Finally, leaders should create an environment that encourages trust and respect, and rewards collaboration and teamwork

Leadership in Resource Constraints

The role of leadership is particularly important when resources are constrained. In these situations, it's easy for teams to become stressed and for communication to break down. Leaders can help by setting clear priorities and providing clear direction. They should focus on motivating the team and helping them to see the bigger picture. They should also work to minimize any politics or bureaucracy that can slow down progress. In addition, leaders should be open to course-correcting when needed. If something isn't working, they should be willing to change the approach and try something new.

Leading by Example

To be an effective leader, it's essential to lead by example. This means that leaders should model the behaviors and values that they want their team to embody. They should be collaborative and open to feedback, and they should put in the same effort that they expect from their team. In addition, leaders should be approachable and willing to listen. It's important to create an environment where team members feel comfortable asking questions and sharing their thoughts. Leaders should also be humble and recognize the strengths of their team members. This will help to create a sense of trust and respect, which is crucial for collaboration.

Motivating Teams during Challenges

When teams are faced with challenges, it's important for leaders to help them stay motivated. It's easy for team members to become discouraged or disengaged, but there are several strategies that leaders can use to help them stay motivated. First, leaders should focus on the team's strengths and accomplishments. They should celebrate successes and recognize hard work. This will help team members to feel appreciated and motivated to continue. Second, leaders should clearly communicate the purpose of the work and how it aligns with the team's goals. This will help to give the team a sense of meaning and purpose.

Decision-making under Limited Resources

The scarcity of resources often means that leaders have to make tough decisions. They must balance competing priorities and make choices that will best benefit the team and the project. There are several techniques that can help leaders make the best possible decisions in these situations. One technique is to use the "80/20 rule." This rule states that 20% of decisions lead to 80% of results. By focusing on the 20% of decisions that will have the biggest impact, leaders can make better use of their limited resources. Another technique is to use a decision matrix.

This early version of Pi can make mistakes. Please don't rely on its information.

Sustainable Growth

Once leaders have helped the team overcome challenges and have made difficult decisions, the next step is to focus on sustainable growth. This means creating a culture that promotes continuous learning and improvement. Leaders should set a vision for the future and help the team see how their work contributes to that vision. They should also encourage team members to take ownership of their work and develop their skills. In addition, leaders should make sure that the team has the resources they need to succeed in the long term. This includes providing training and development opportunities and ensuring that the team has the tools and equipment they need to do their jobs effectively.

This early version of Pi can make mistakes. Please don't rely on its information.

Balancing Growth and Resource
Constraints
development with the limitations of available resources. This balancing act can be difficult, but there are several things that leaders can do to find the right balance. First, they should prioritize projects based on their impact and feasibility. Second, they should seek opportunities to leverage existing resources to accomplish more. For example, they could look for ways to automate processes or share resources across teams. Finally, leaders should be open to finding creative solutions and

out-of-the-box thinking. This can lead to innovative ways to overcome resource constraints.

Long-term Planning for Success

When it comes to long-term planning, leaders should focus on both short-term and long-term goals. Short-term goals should be realistic and achievable, while long-term goals should be ambitious and challenging. To ensure long-term success, leaders should:

Regularly reassess the team's progress and adjust plans accordingly.

Continuously monitor the team's strengths and weaknesses and provide appropriate support.

Keep the team's vision front and center, even in times of change or uncertainty.

Encourage the team to take risks and experiment with new ideas.

Building Resilience

Resilience is the ability to bounce back from challenges and setbacks, and it's a crucial skill for teams to develop. Leaders can help build resilience by:

Encouraging open and honest communication.

Creating a culture of support and trust.

Prioritizing self-care and work-life balance.

Providing opportunities for growth and development.

Creating a positive work environment where mistakes are seen as learning opportunities.

Being honest and transparent about challenges and setbacks.

Personal Productivity

pay attention to their own personal productivity. This includes:

Setting priorities and goals for themselves, just like they do for the team.

Managing their time effectively and avoiding distractions.

Taking care of their own well-being, both mentally and physically.

Identifying their own strengths and weaknesses, and working to improve them.

Taking the time to learn and grow as a leader.

Personal productivity is essential for leaders, as it helps them to set a good example for the team and to lead with clarity and confidence.

Applying Efficiency Principles to Personal Life

better balance between their work and personal lives and become more resilient and productive overall. Leaders can:

Track and analyze how they spend their time.

Set boundaries between work and personal life.

Identify personal goals and work towards them.

Allow themselves to rest and recharge.

Prioritize their health and well-being.

Practice gratitude and appreciation for their life and work.

Be intentional about their time and choices.

Work-Life Balance

Work-life balance is an important aspect of personal productivity and well-being. It involves finding a balance between the time and energy spent on work and the time and energy spent on personal life. When leaders prioritize their work-life balance, they can avoid burnout and perform better in both their personal and professional lives. However, finding the right balance can be challenging and requires constant effort and adjustment. Leaders can:

Review their priorities and adjust them as needed.

Learn to say "no" to things that don't align with their goals.

Make time for the things that bring them joy and fulfillment.

Self-Care and Well-being

A key component of work-life balance is self-care and well-being. Leaders should prioritize taking care of their physical and mental health. This can include:

Getting enough sleep.

Eating a healthy diet.

Getting regular exercise.

Making time for hobbies and relaxation.

Practicing mindfulness.

Connecting with loved ones.

Managing stress levels.

By taking care of themselves, leaders can better take care of their team and achieve their goals.

Conclusion
Recap of Key Points Doing More with Less:

In summary, here are the key points of "doing more with less":

Prioritize the most important tasks.

Streamline processes and eliminate waste.

Seek innovative solutions.

Build resilience.

Focus on work-life balance.

Take care of yourself.

Remember that "less" does not mean "nothing." It's about being intentional and focused on the most important things

www.ingramcontent.com/pod-product-compliance
Lightning Source LLC
Chambersburg PA
CBHW072230290526
45794CB00007B/2958